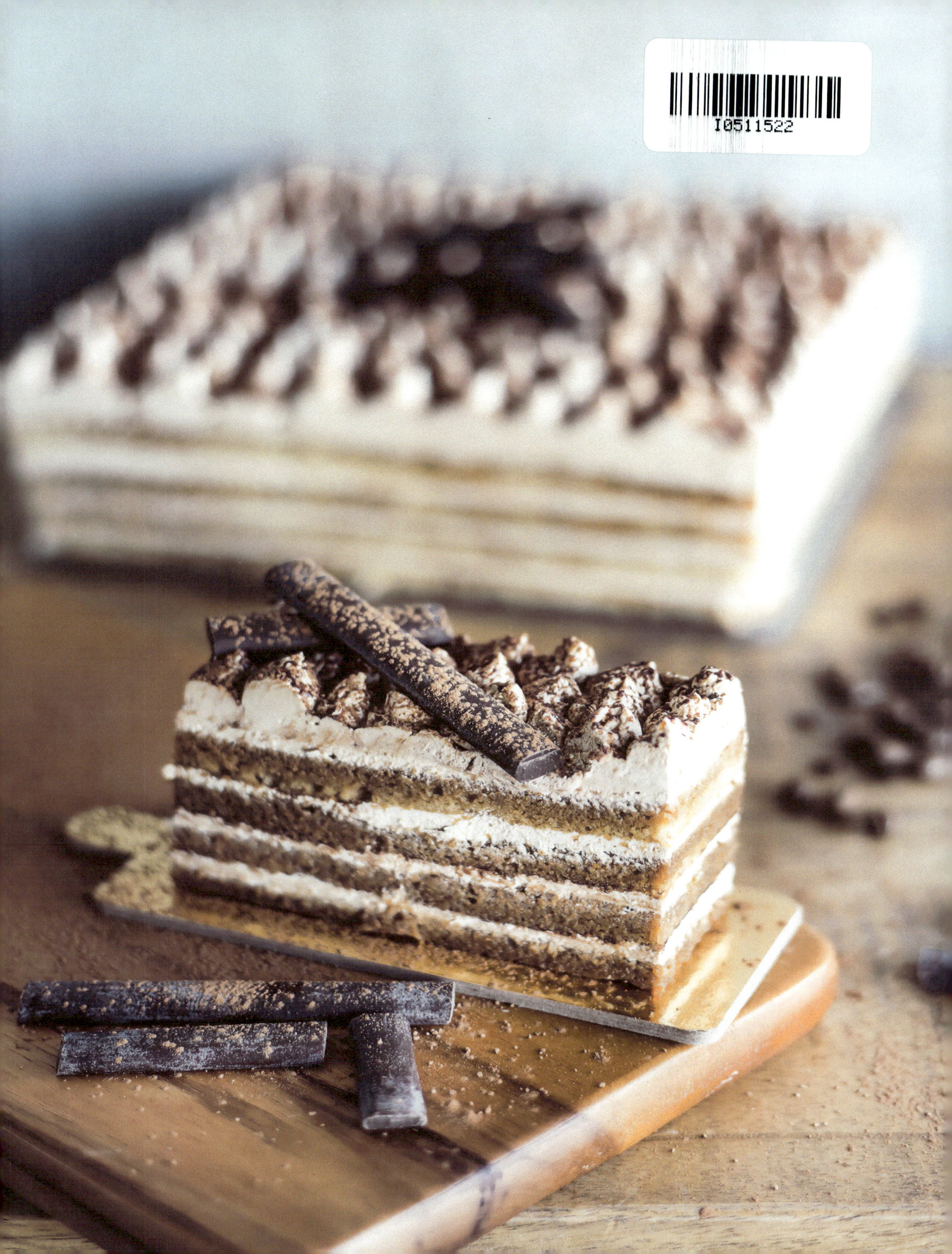

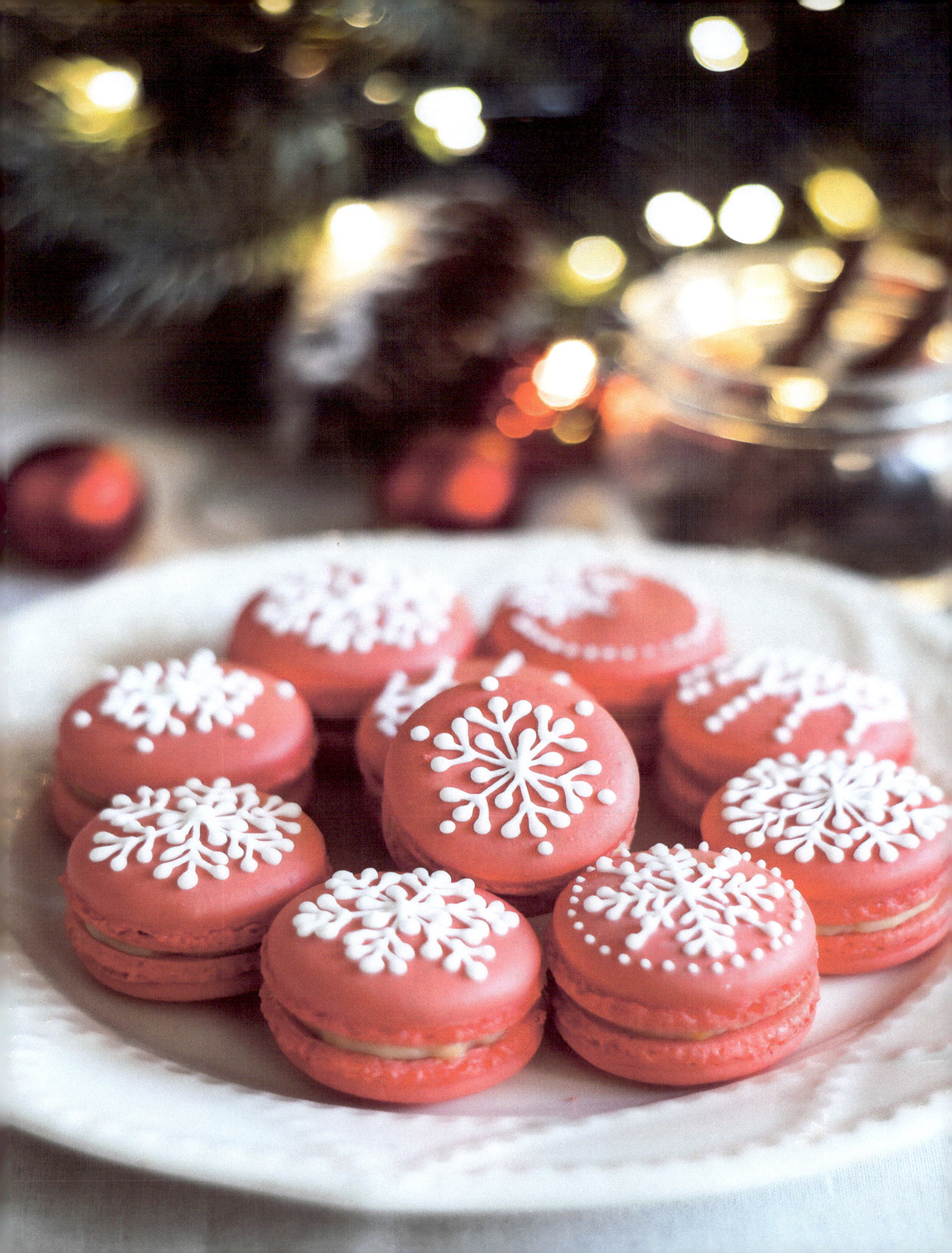

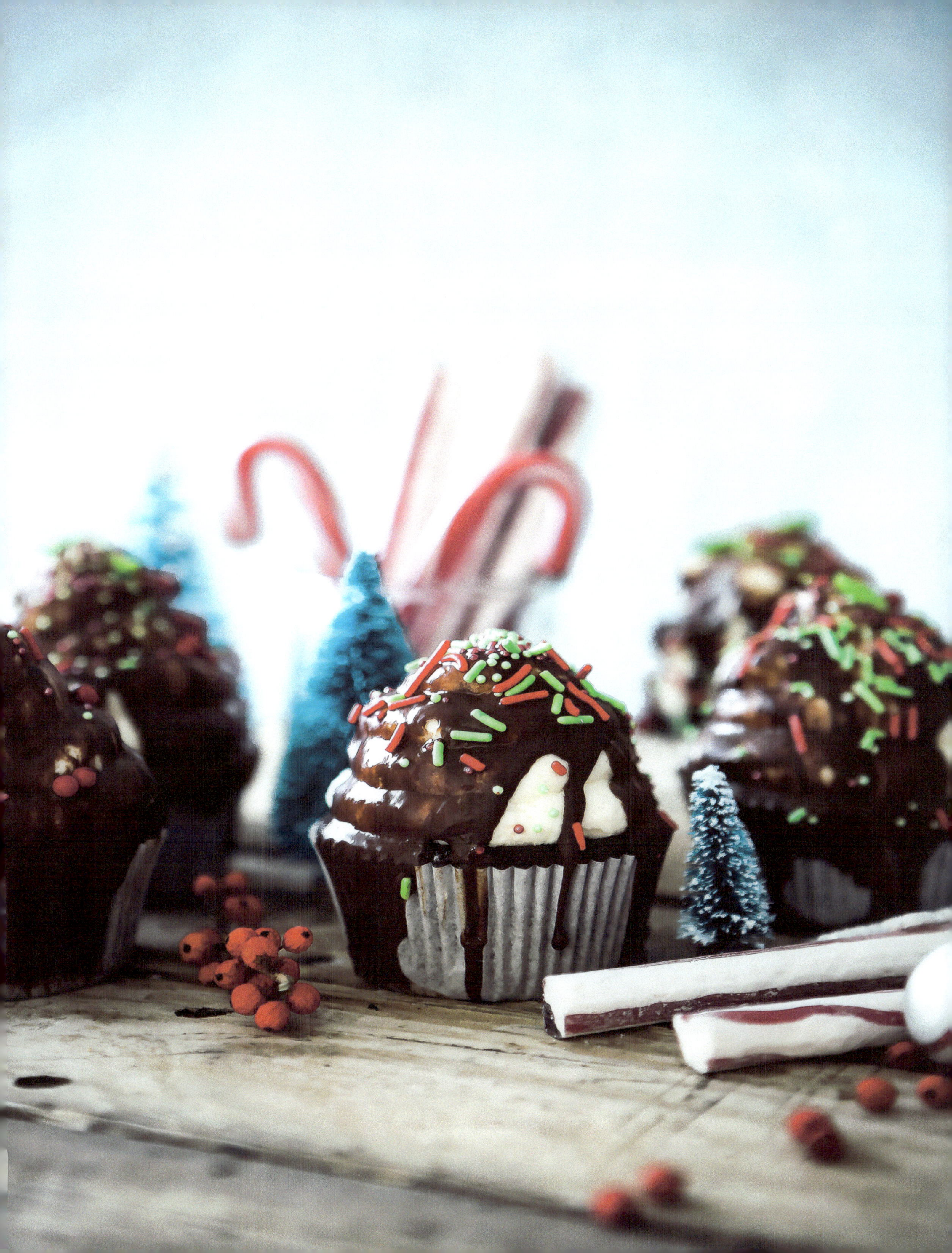

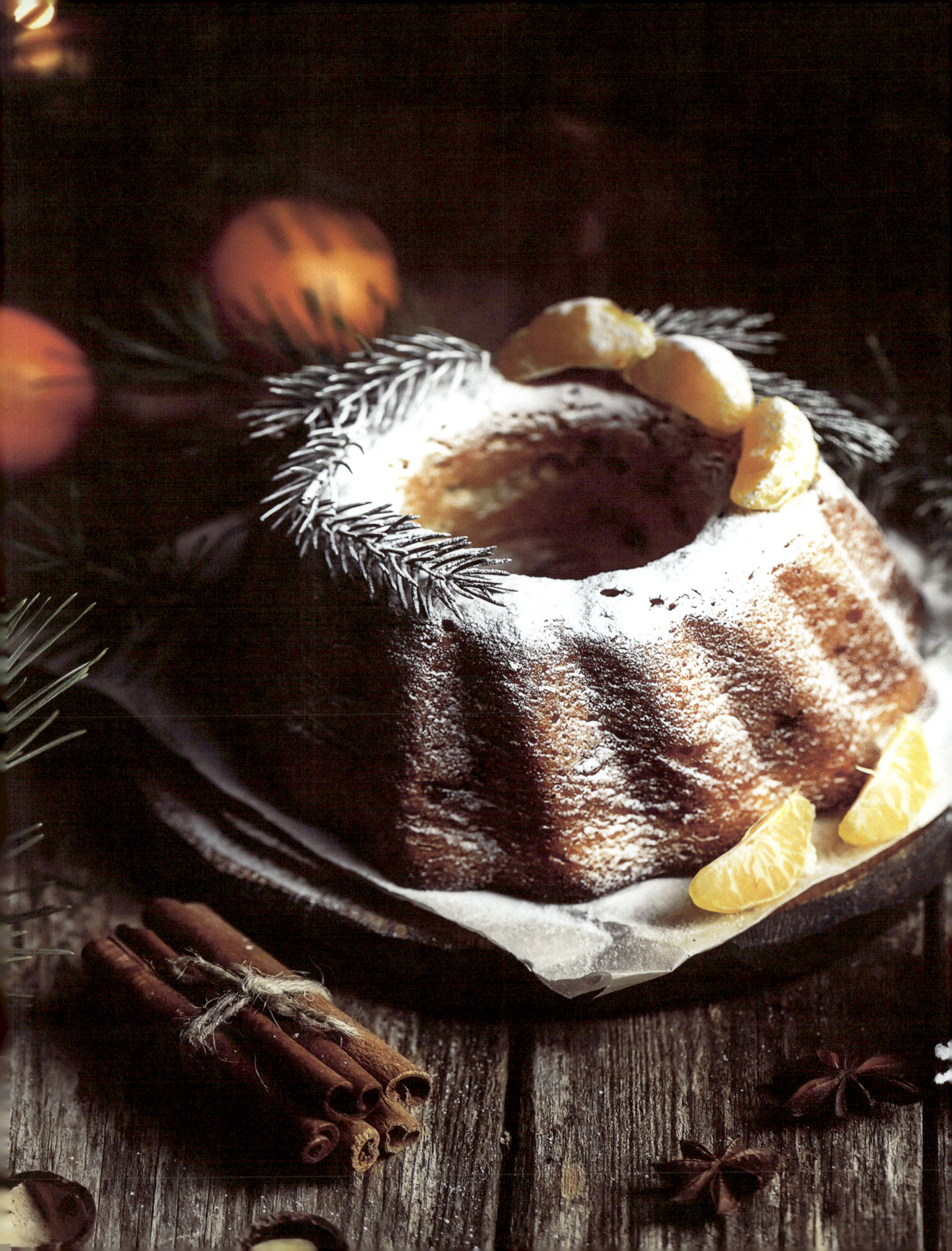

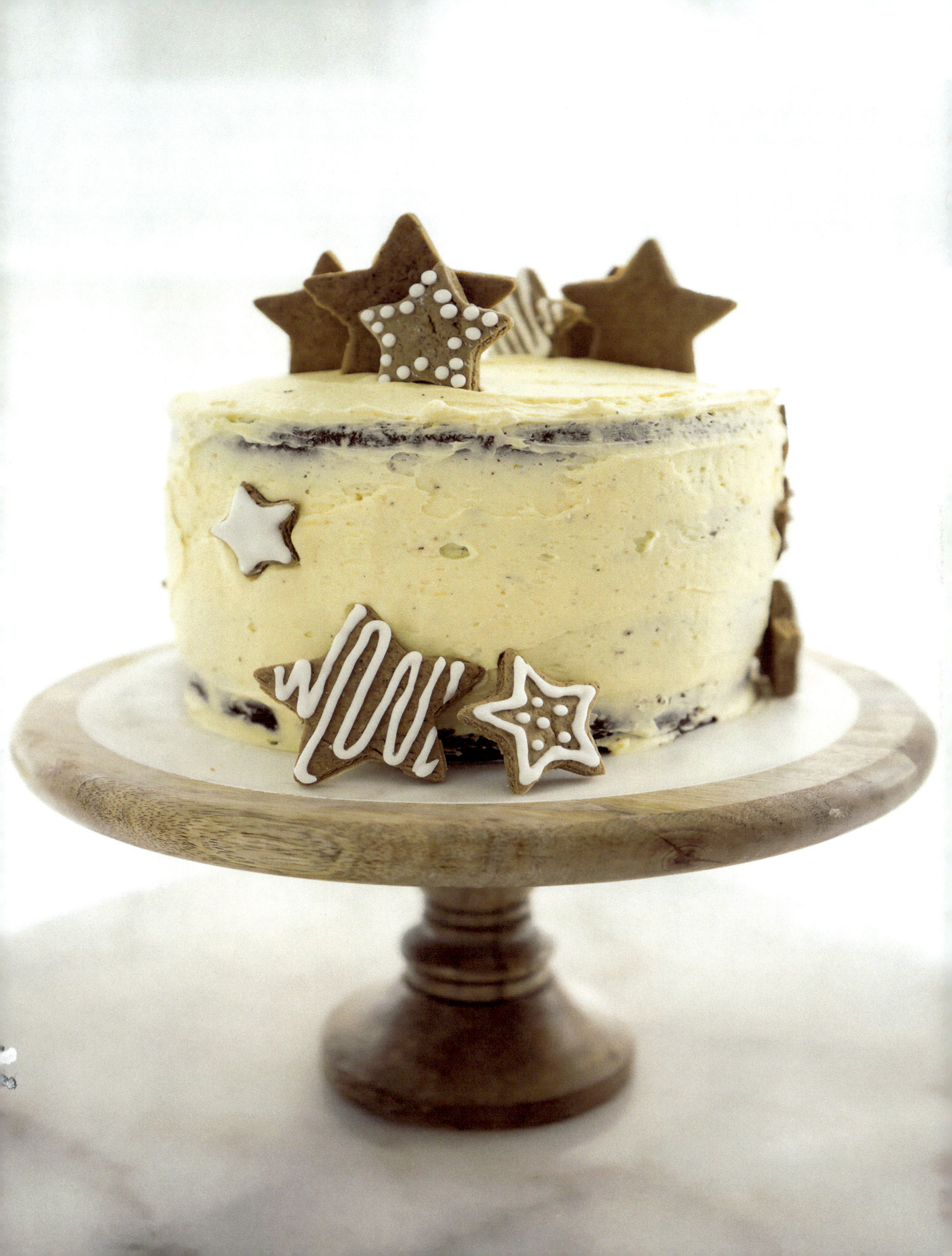

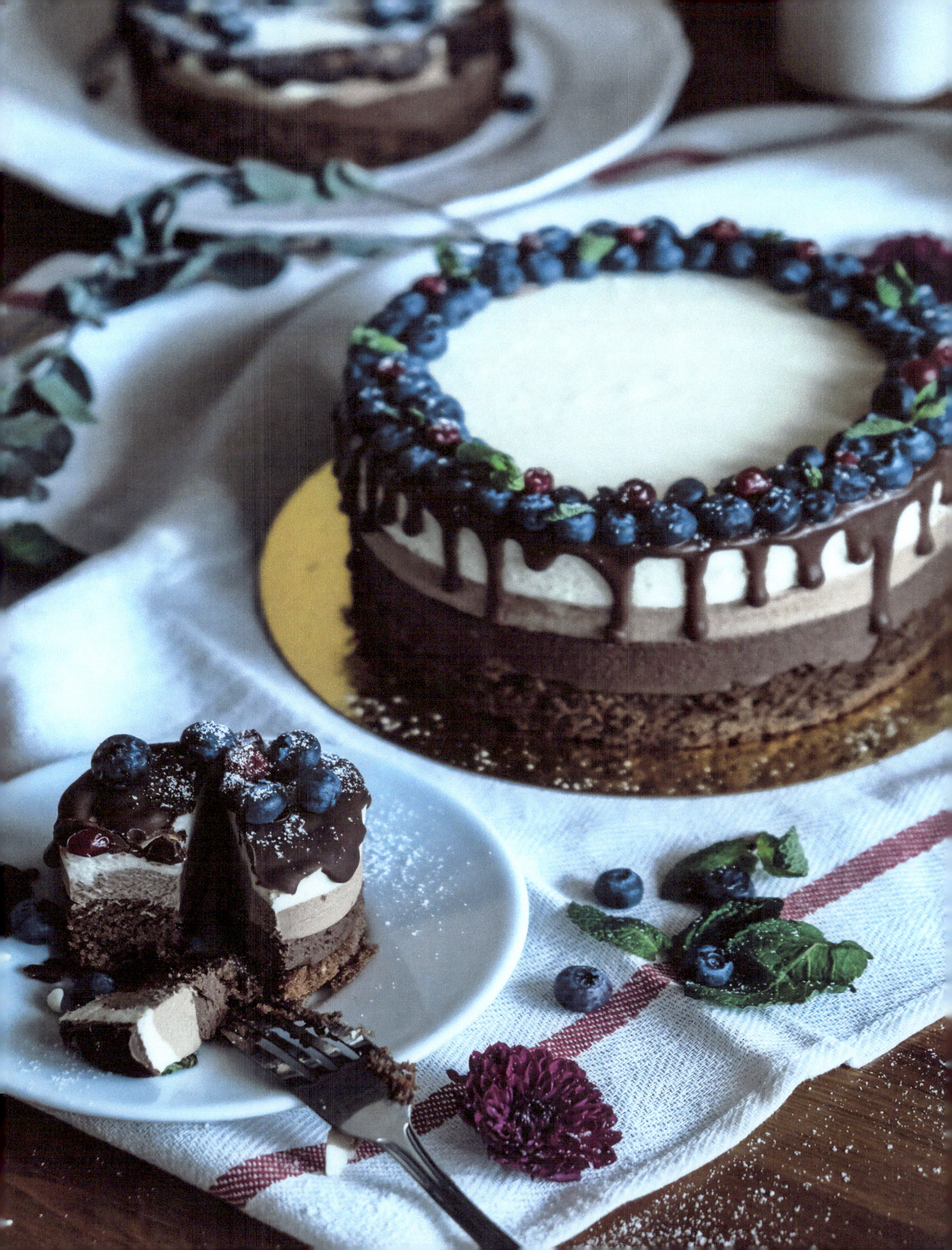

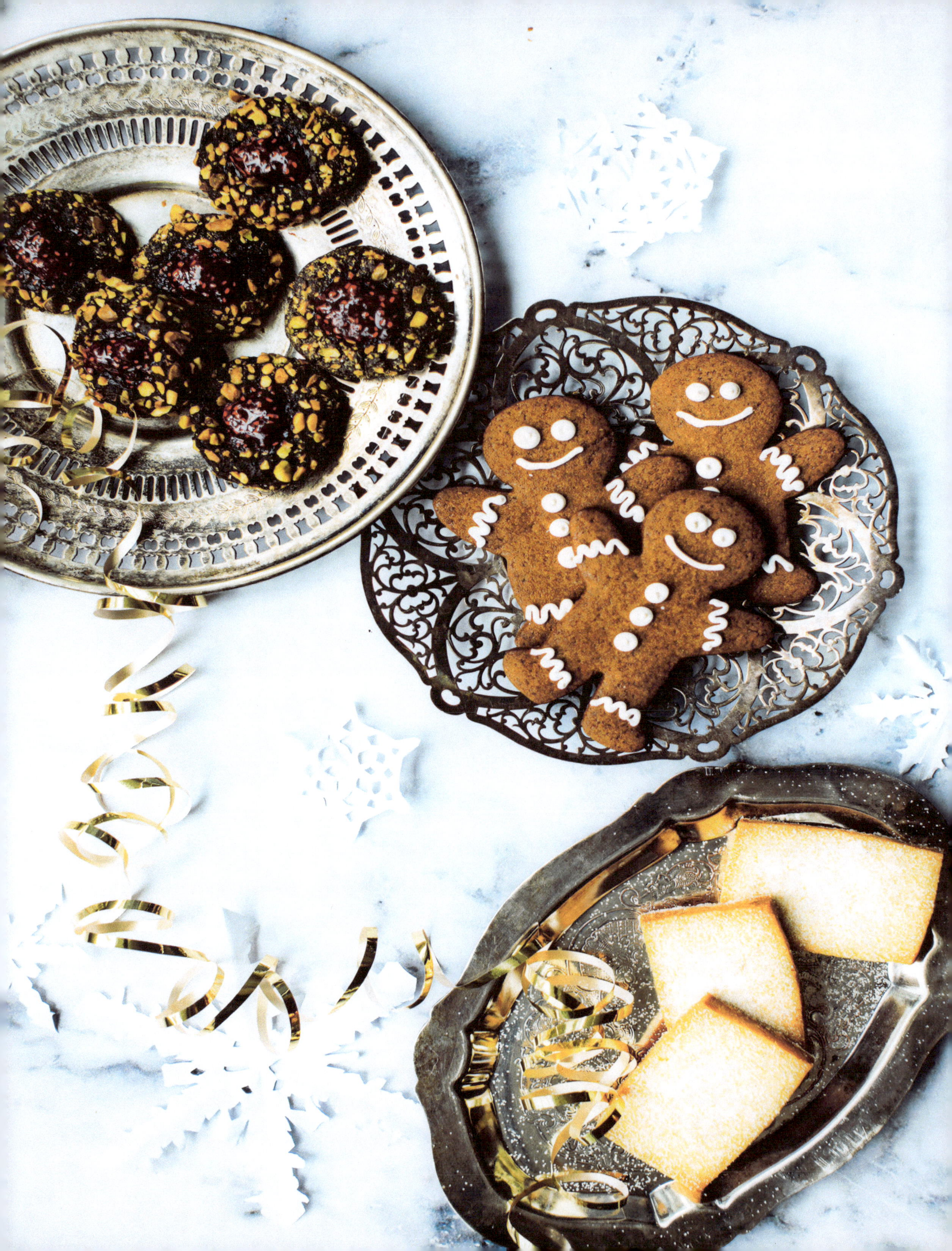

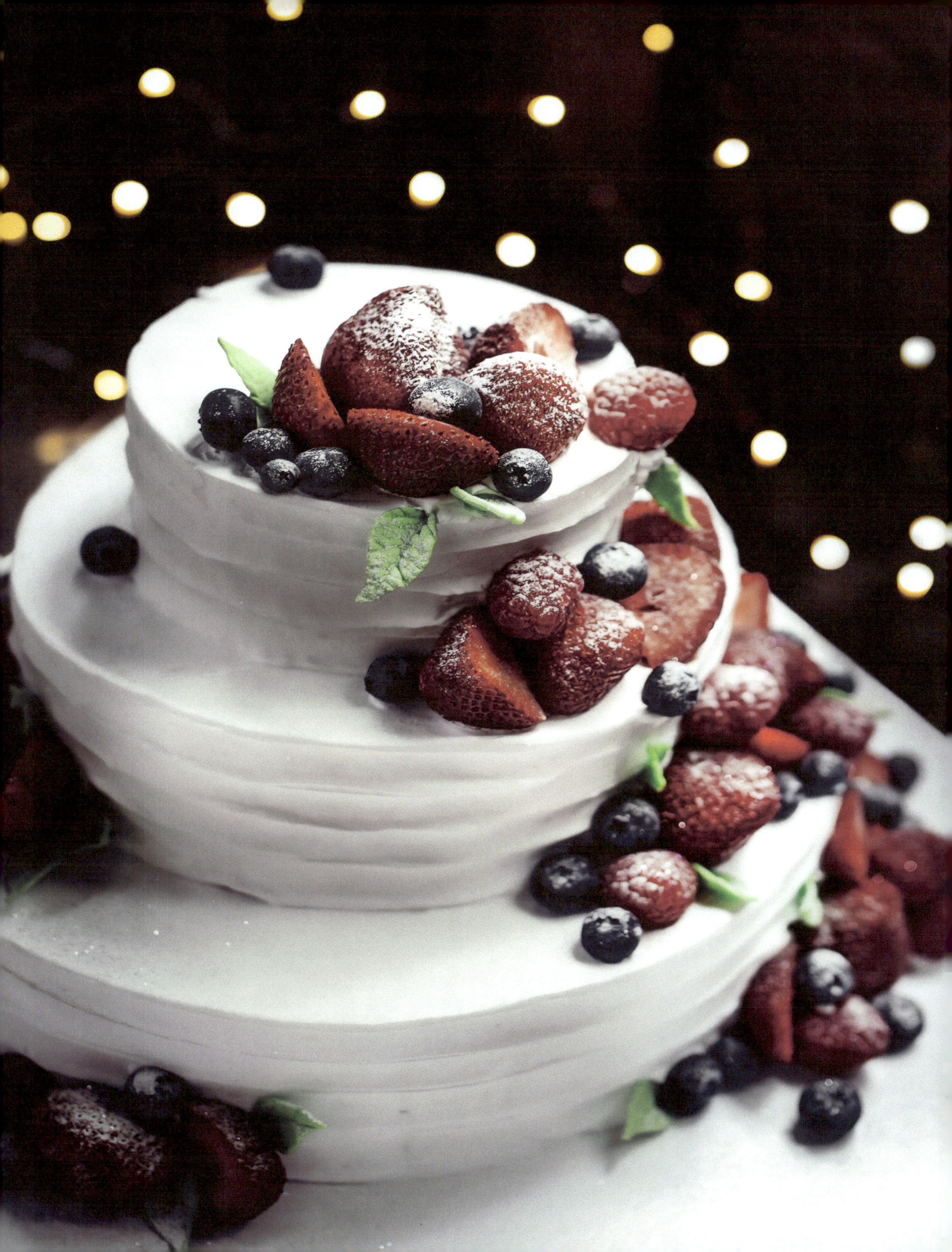

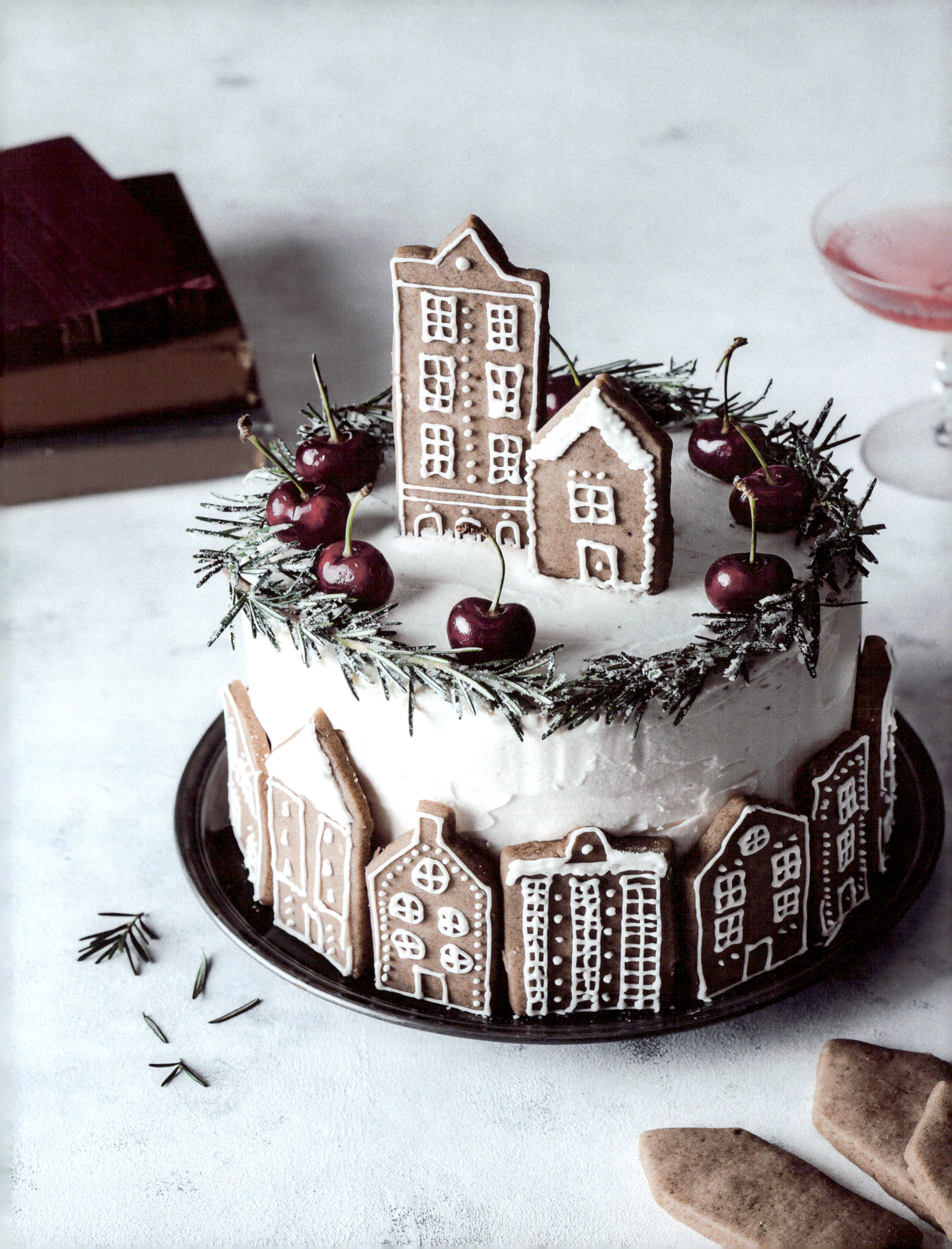

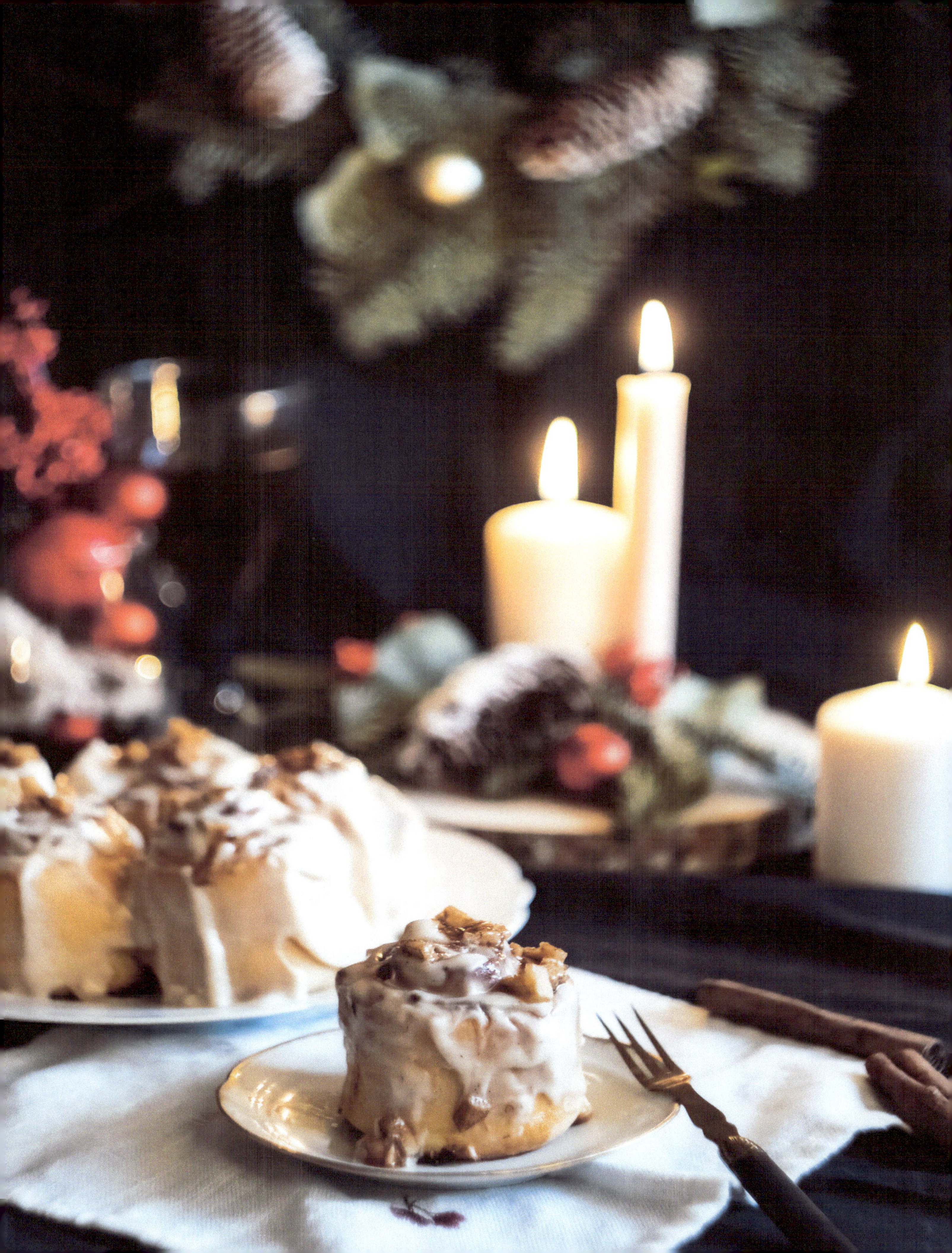

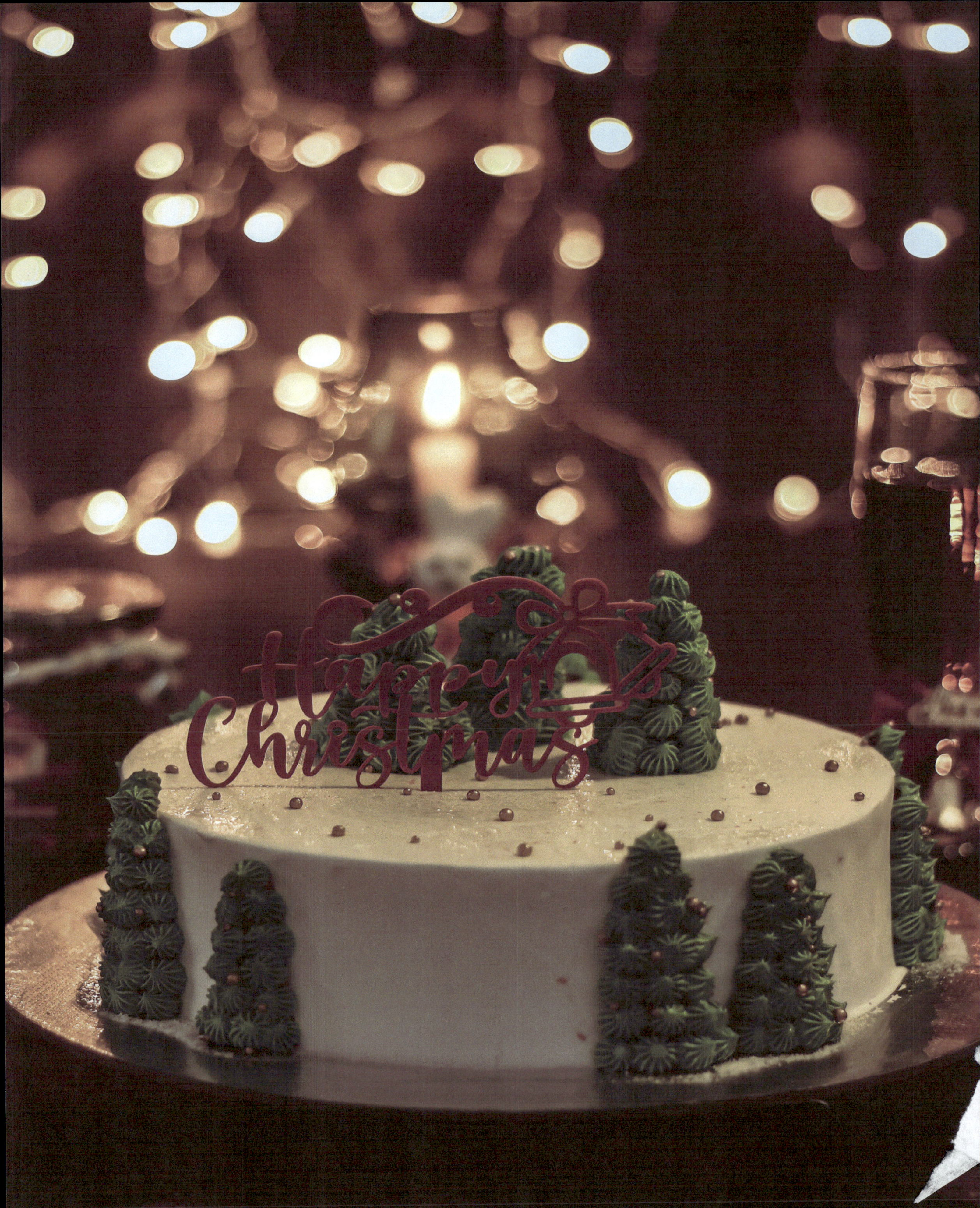
Happy
Christmas

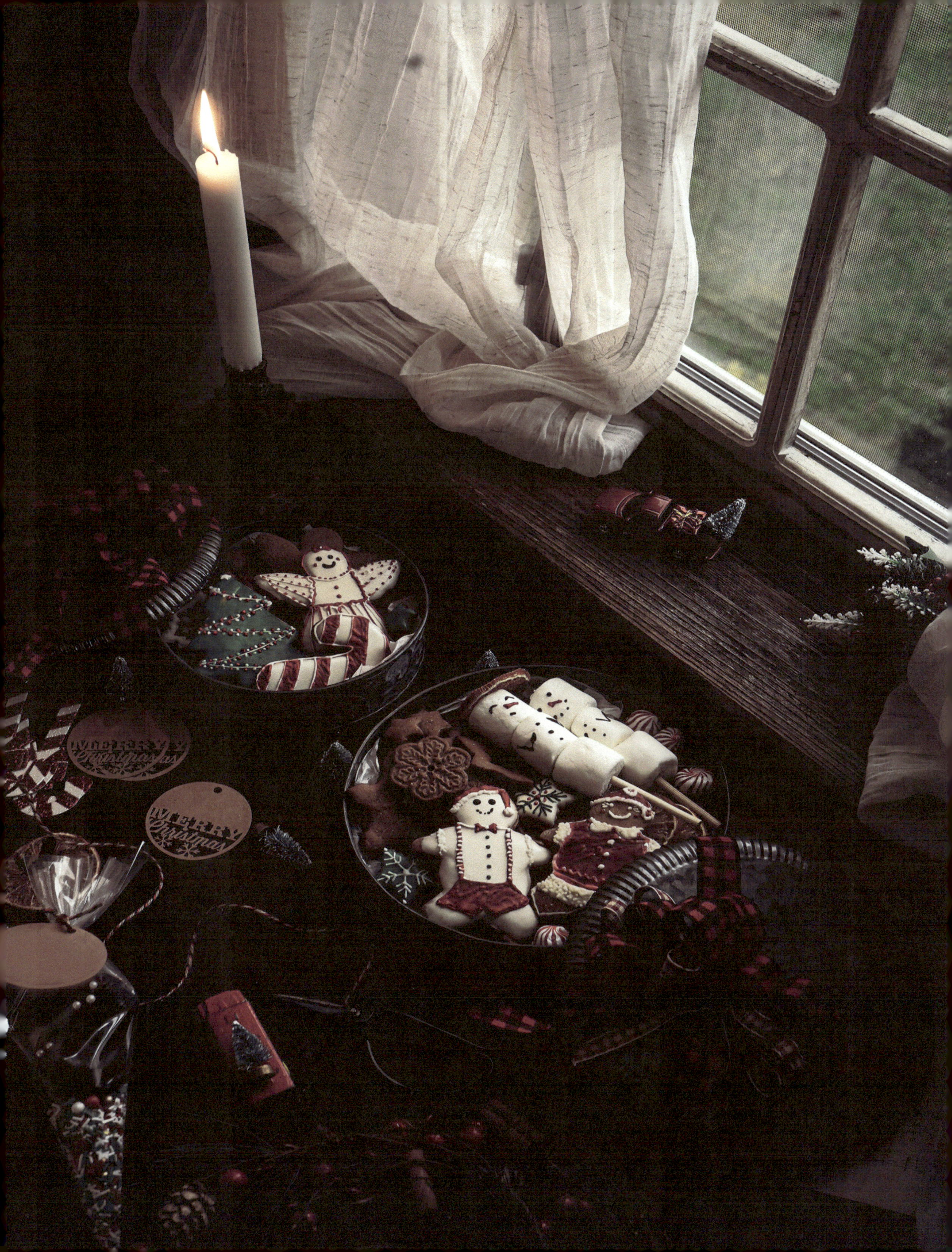
MERRY Christmas
MERRY Christmas

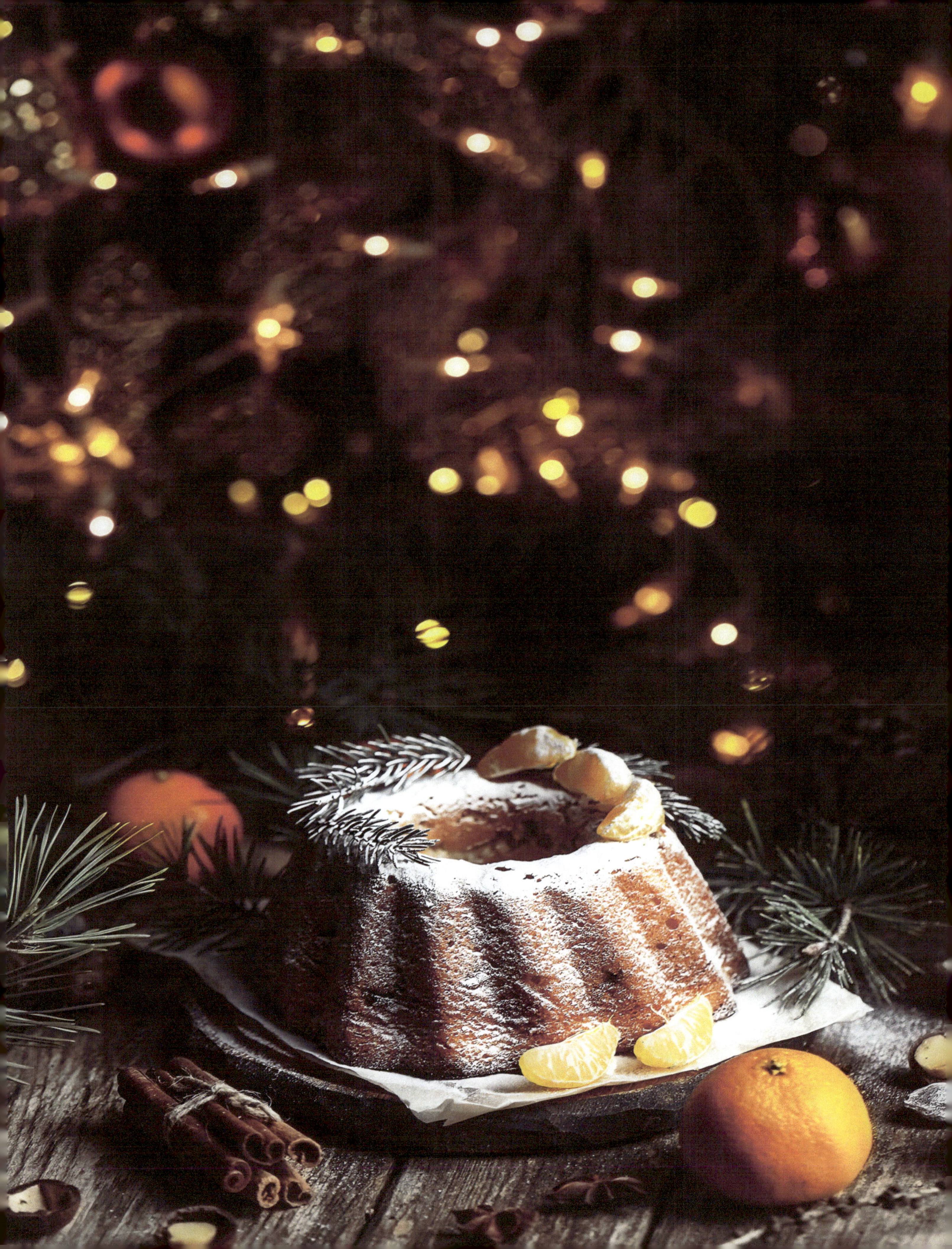

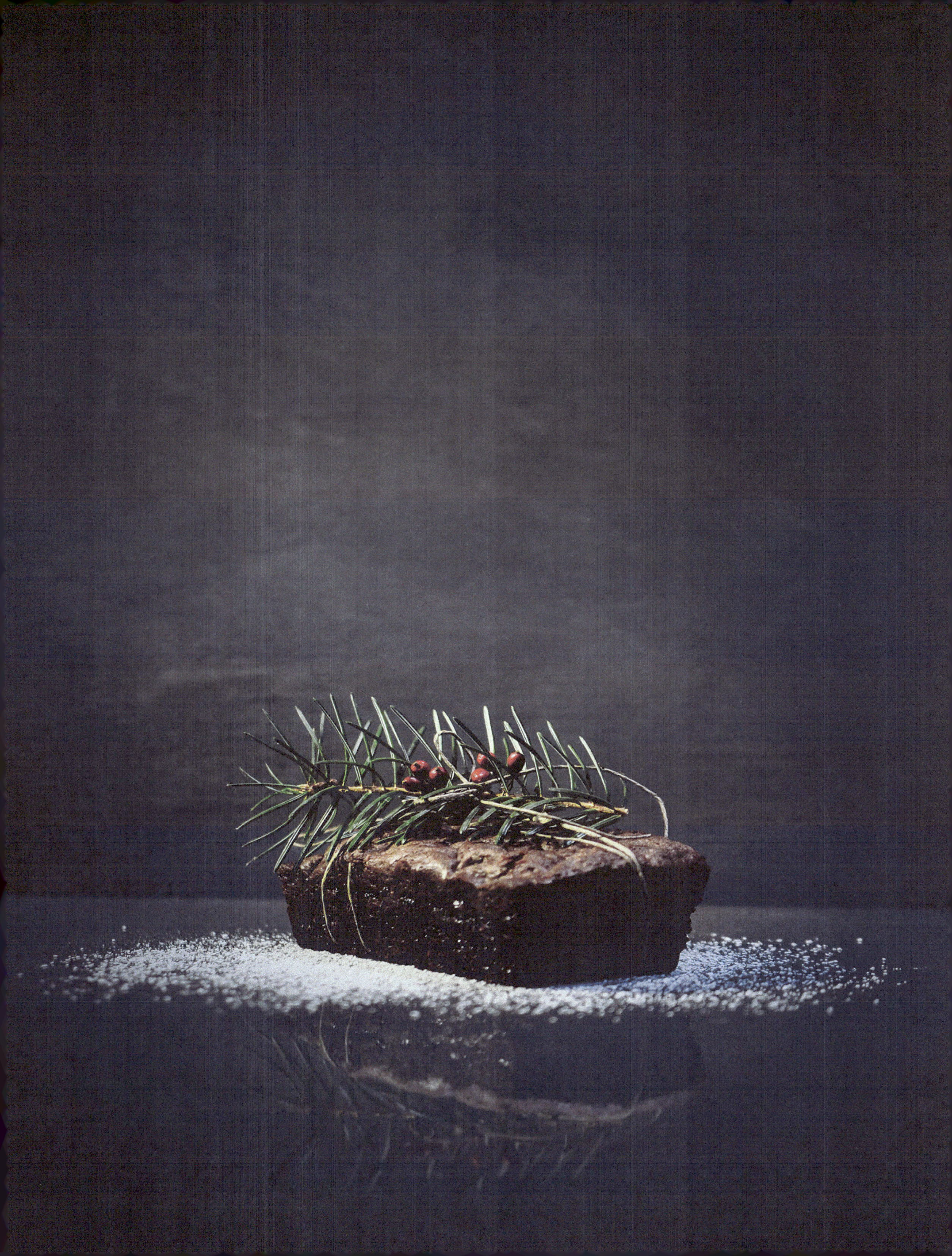

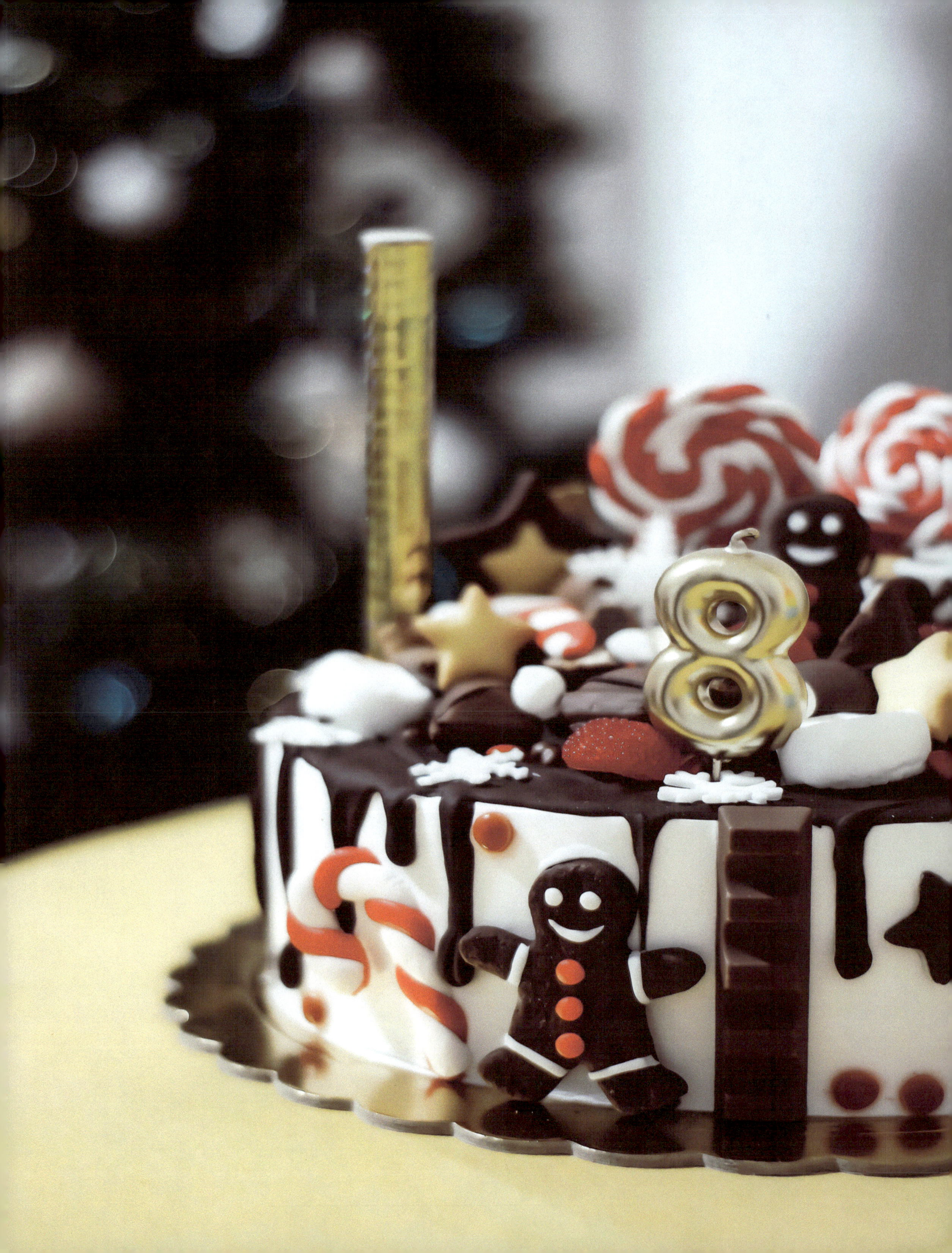

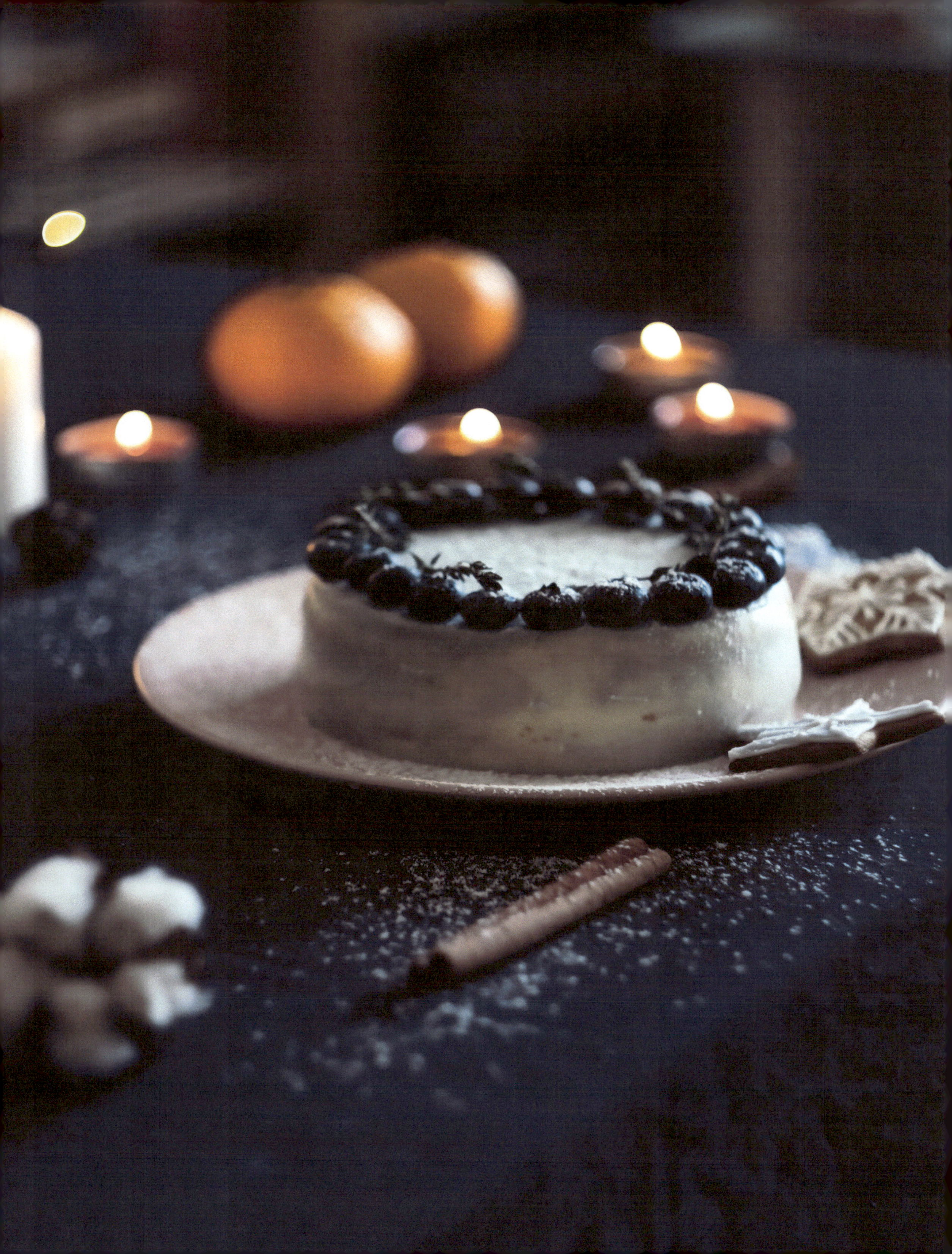

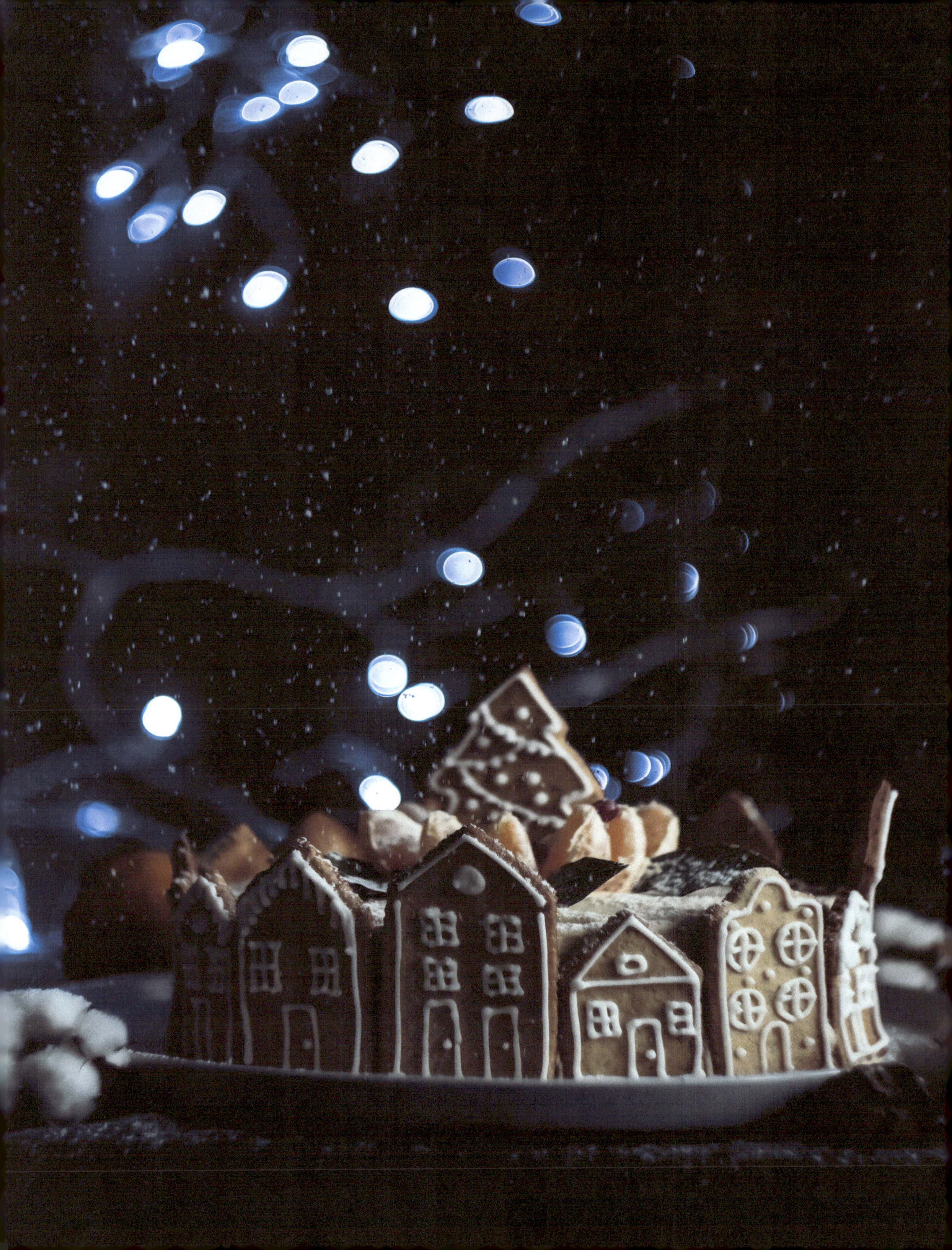

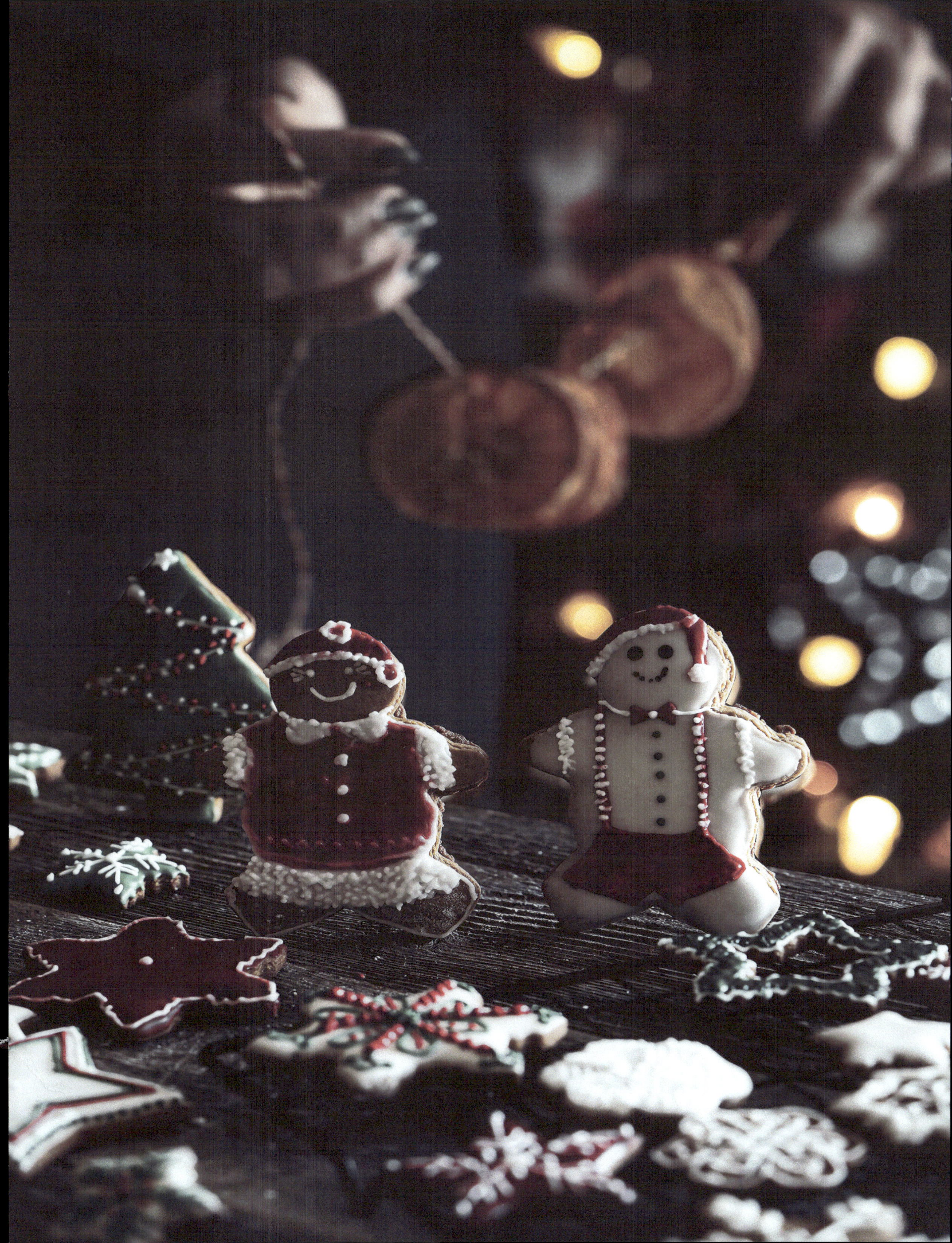

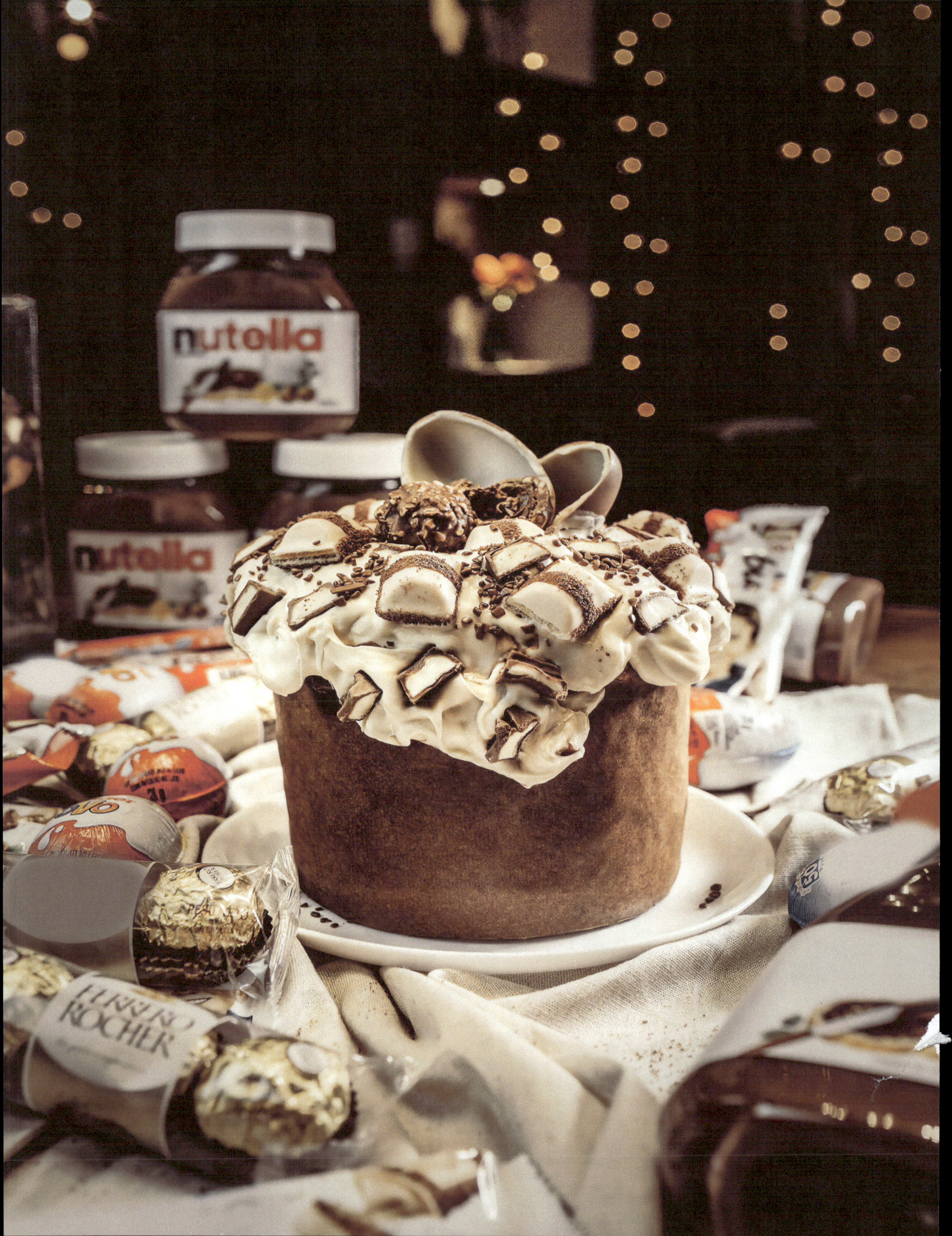
nutella
nutella
FERRERO ROCHER

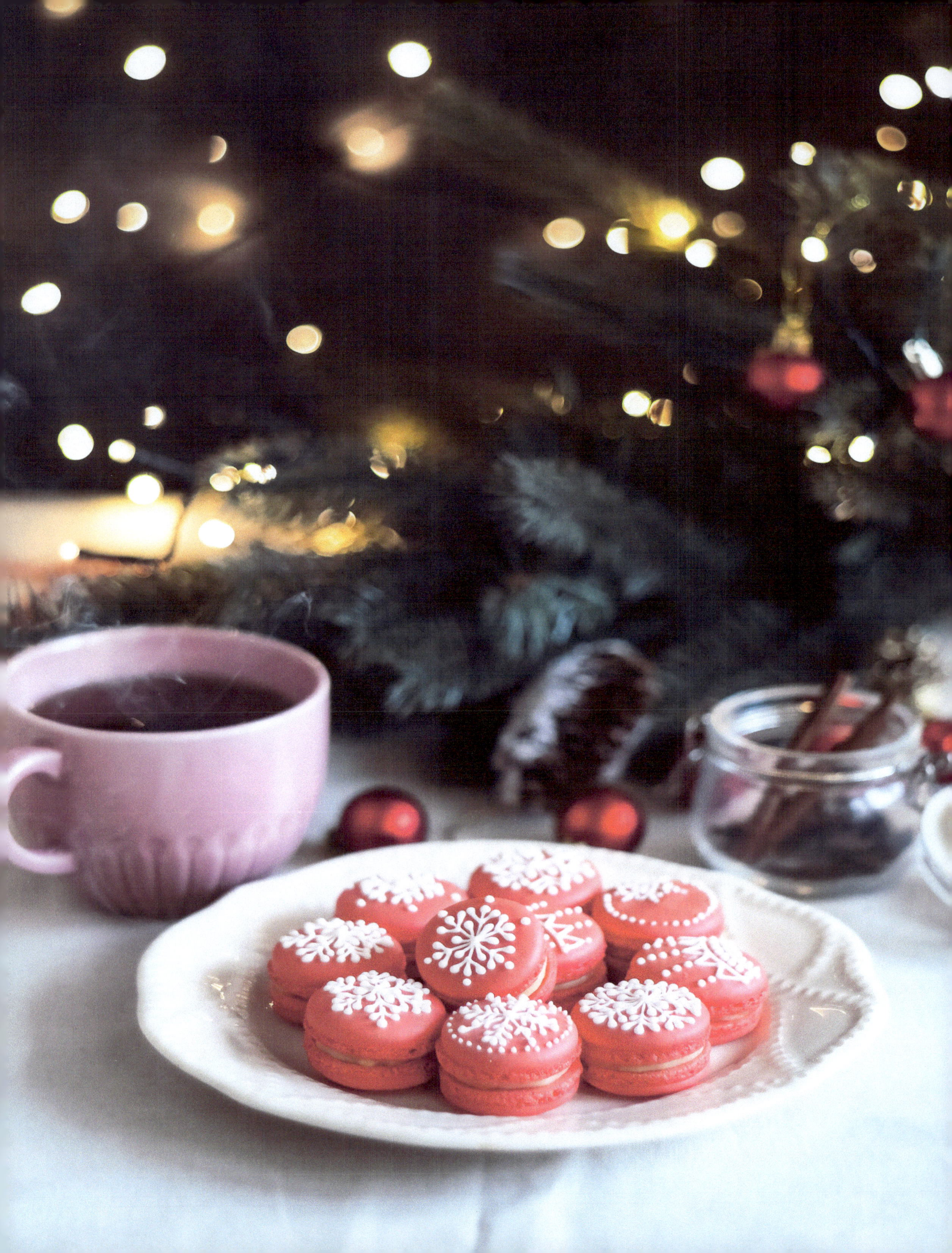

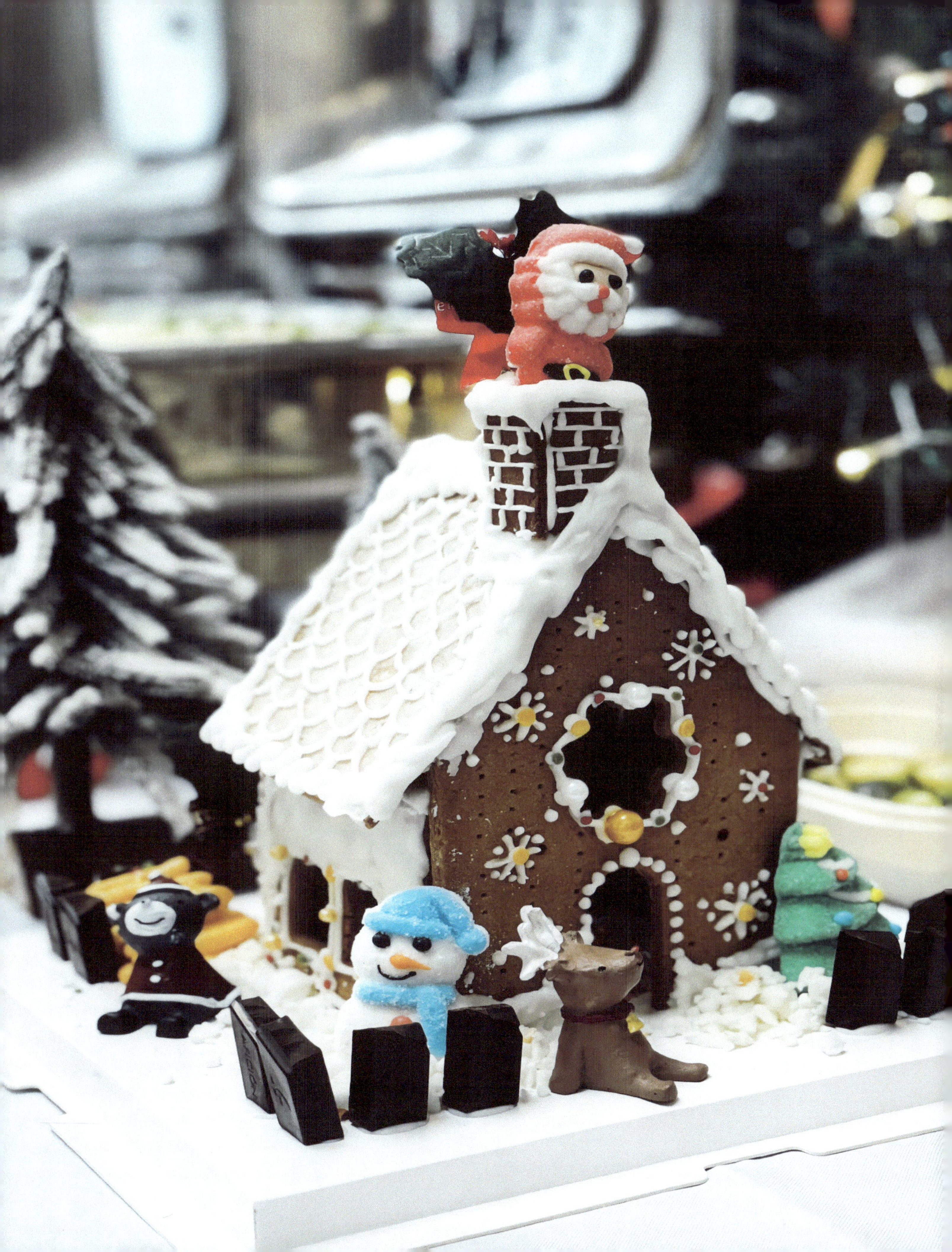

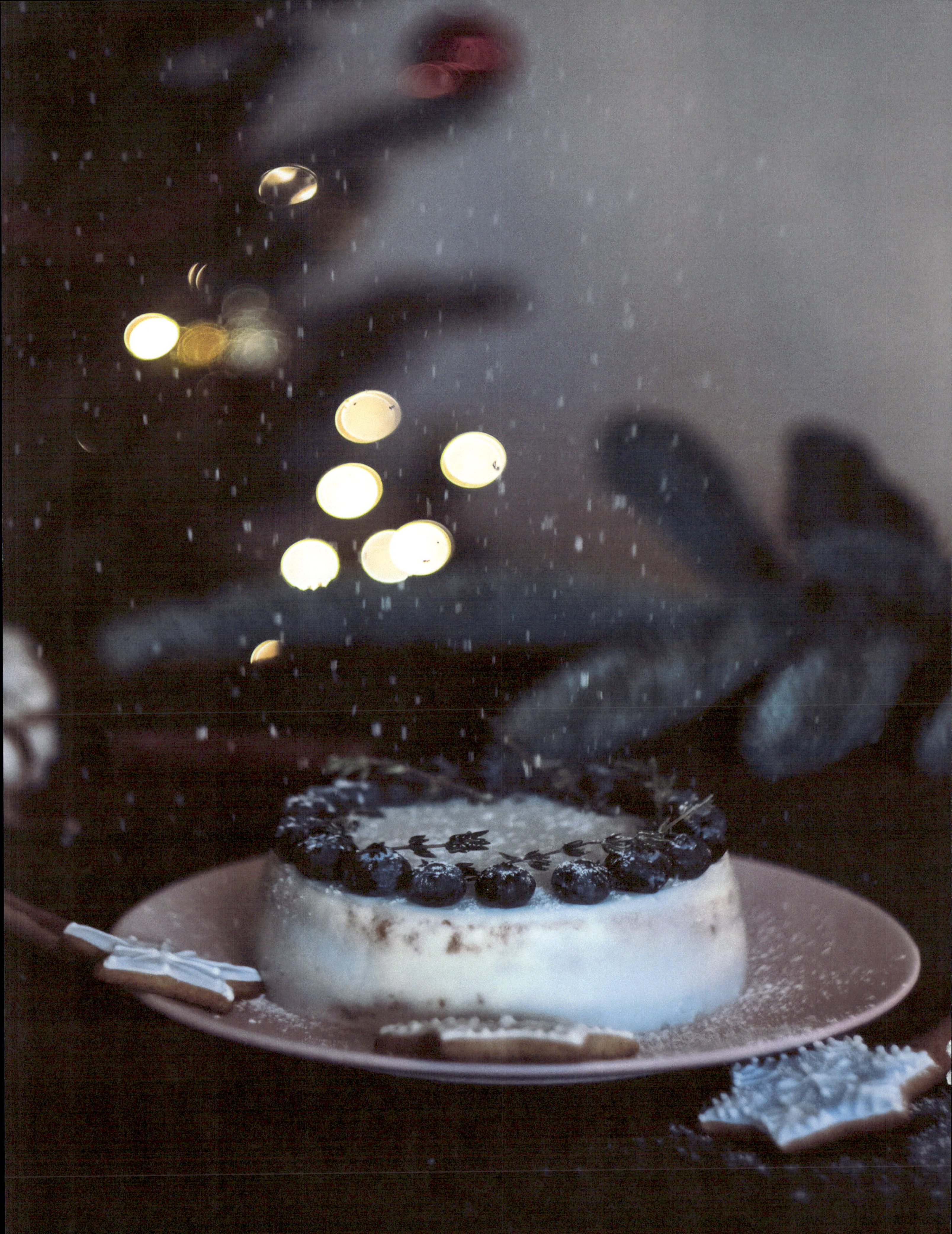

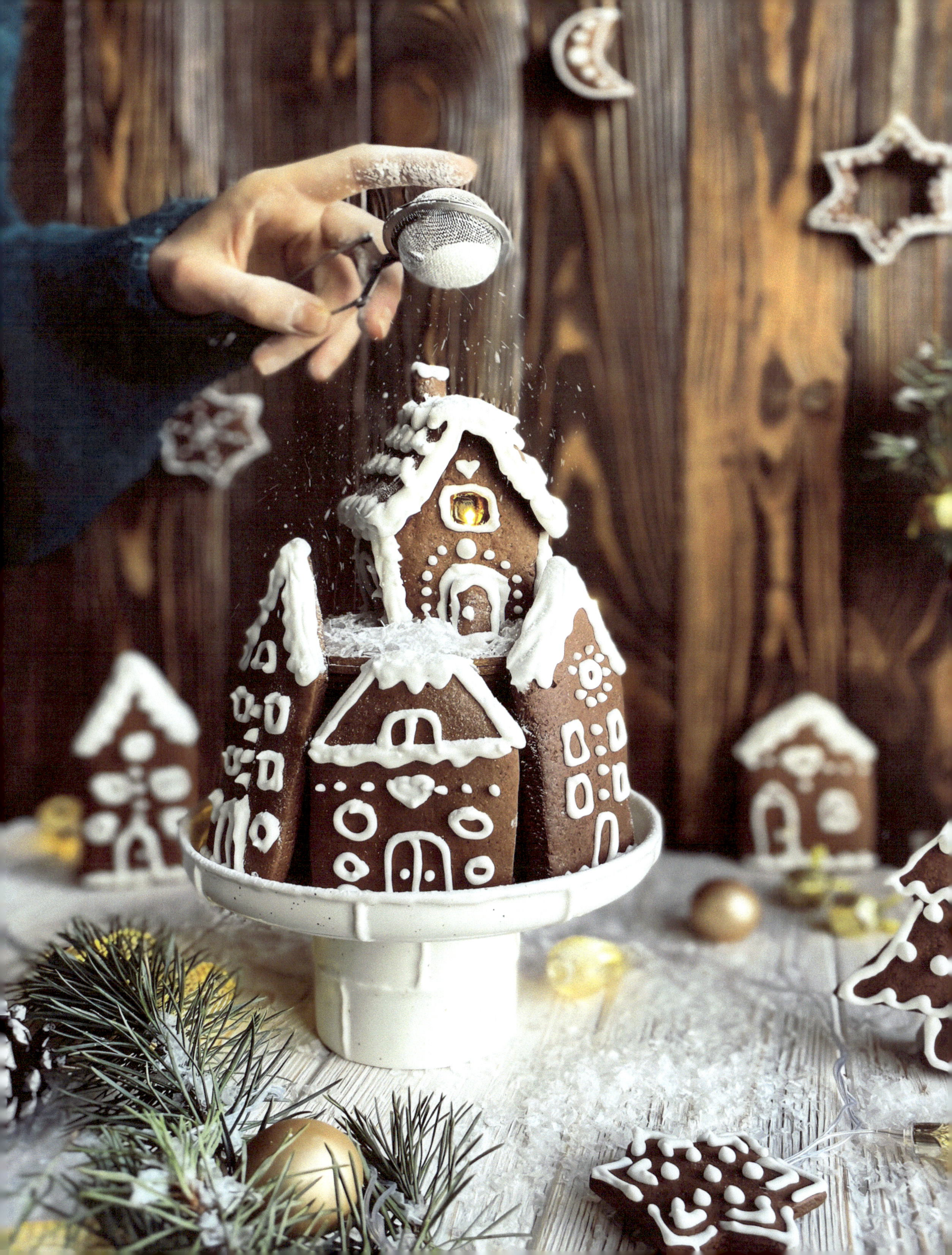

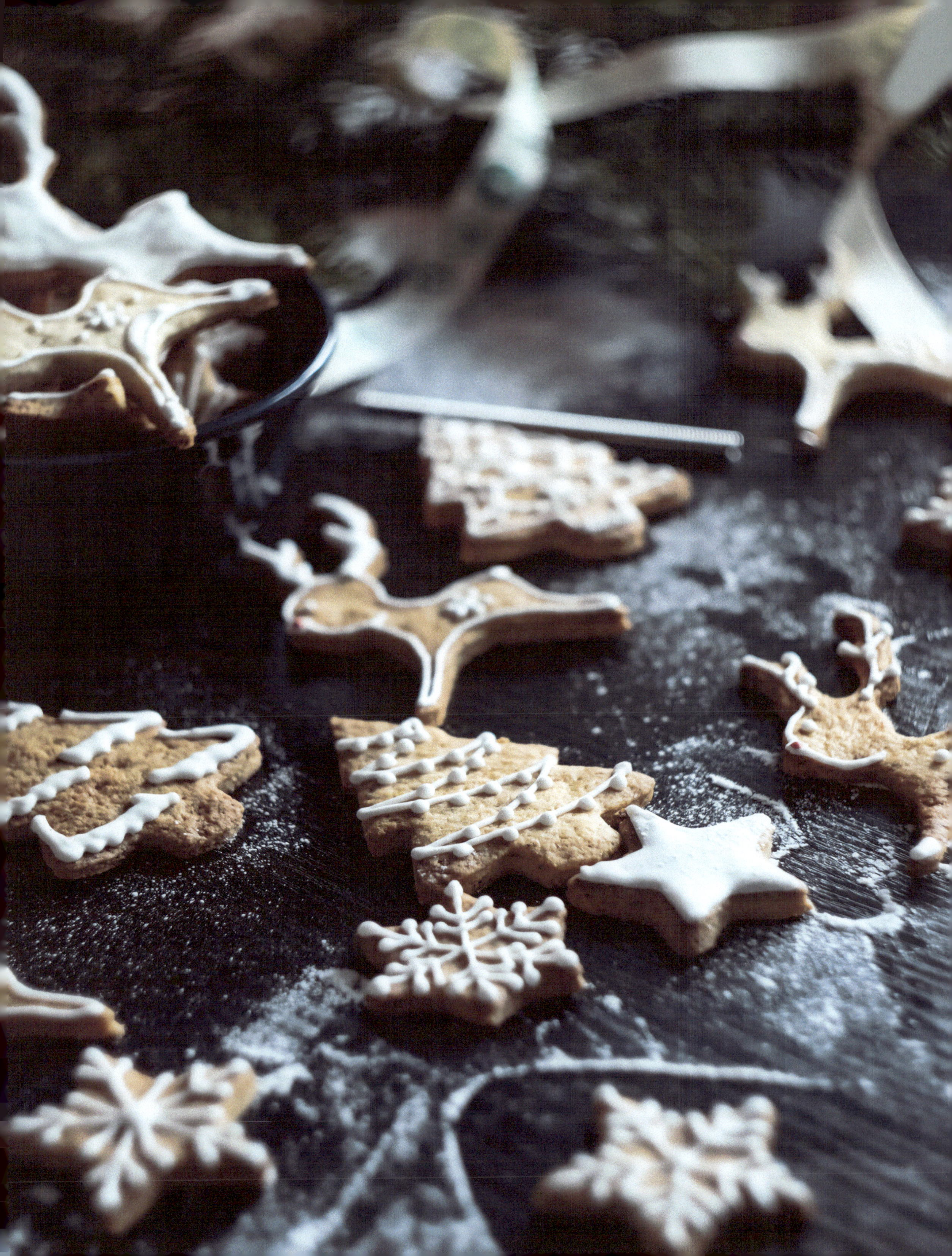

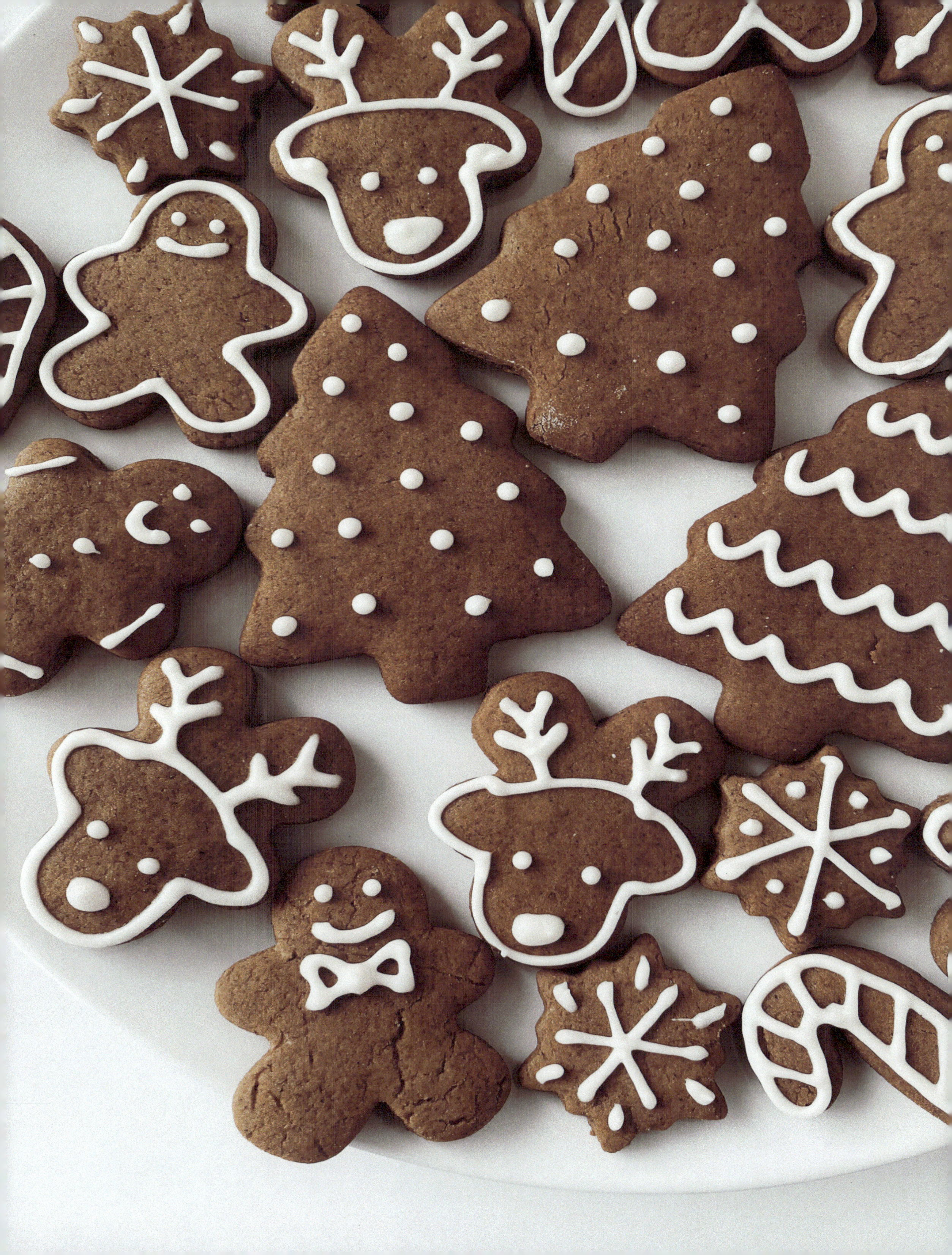

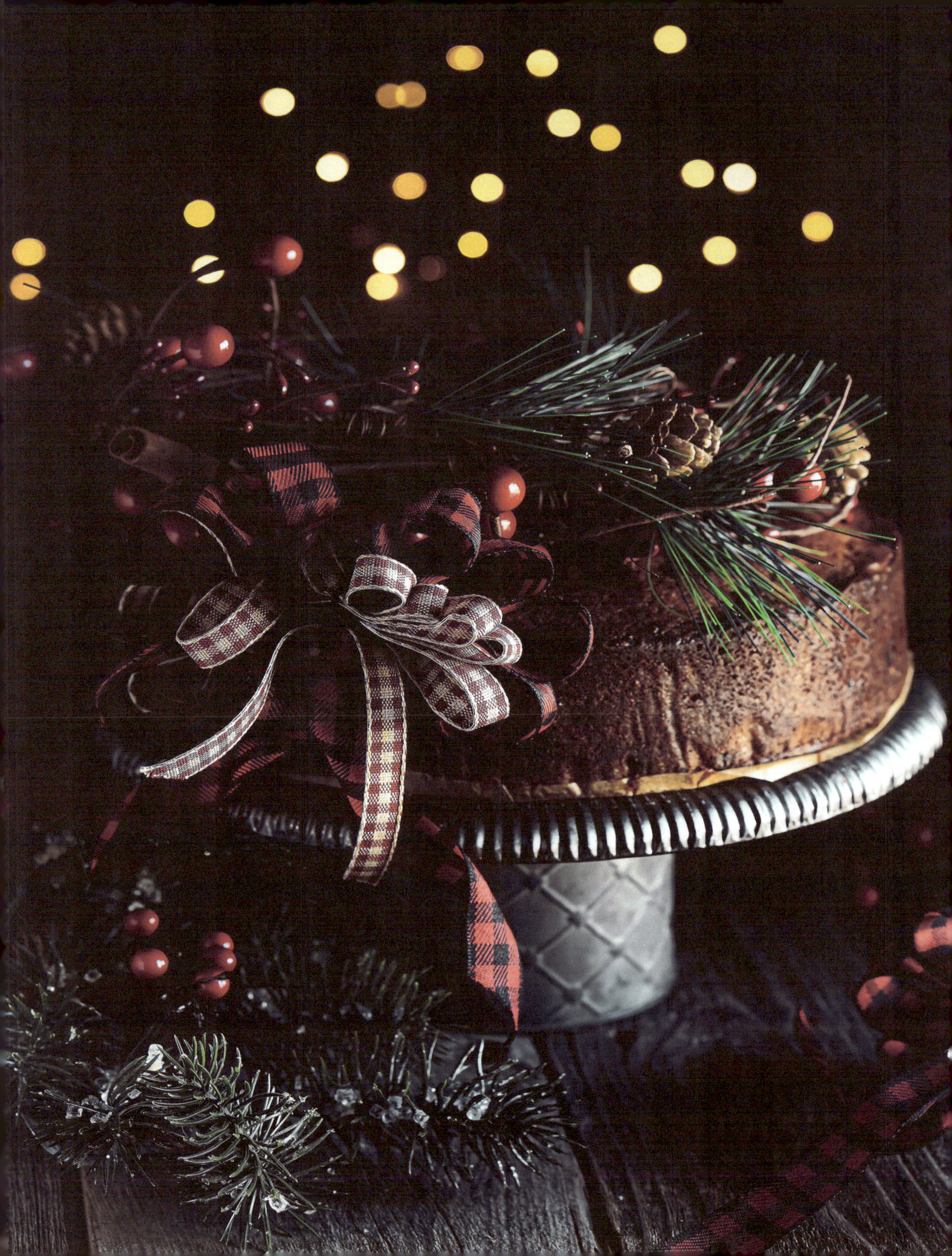

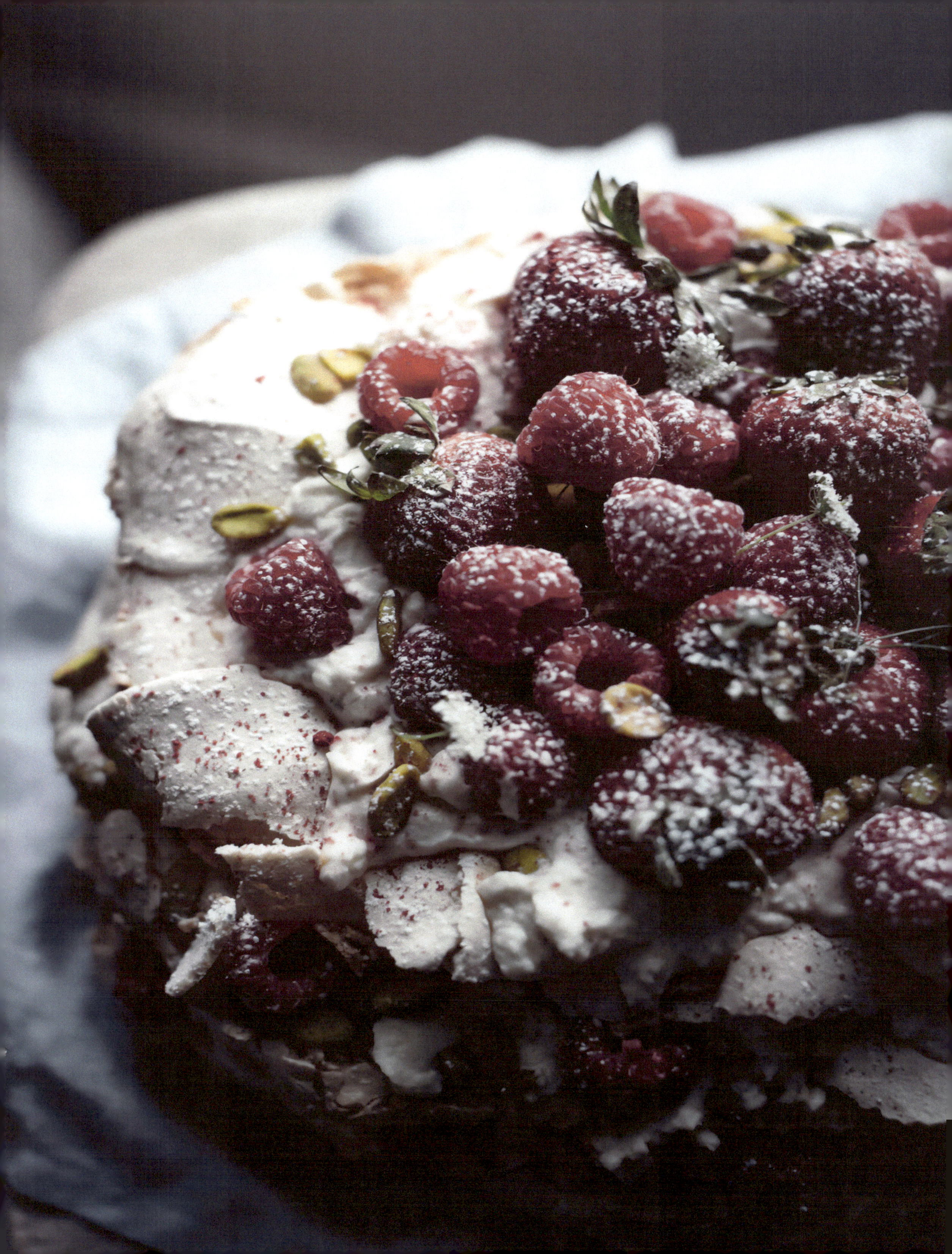

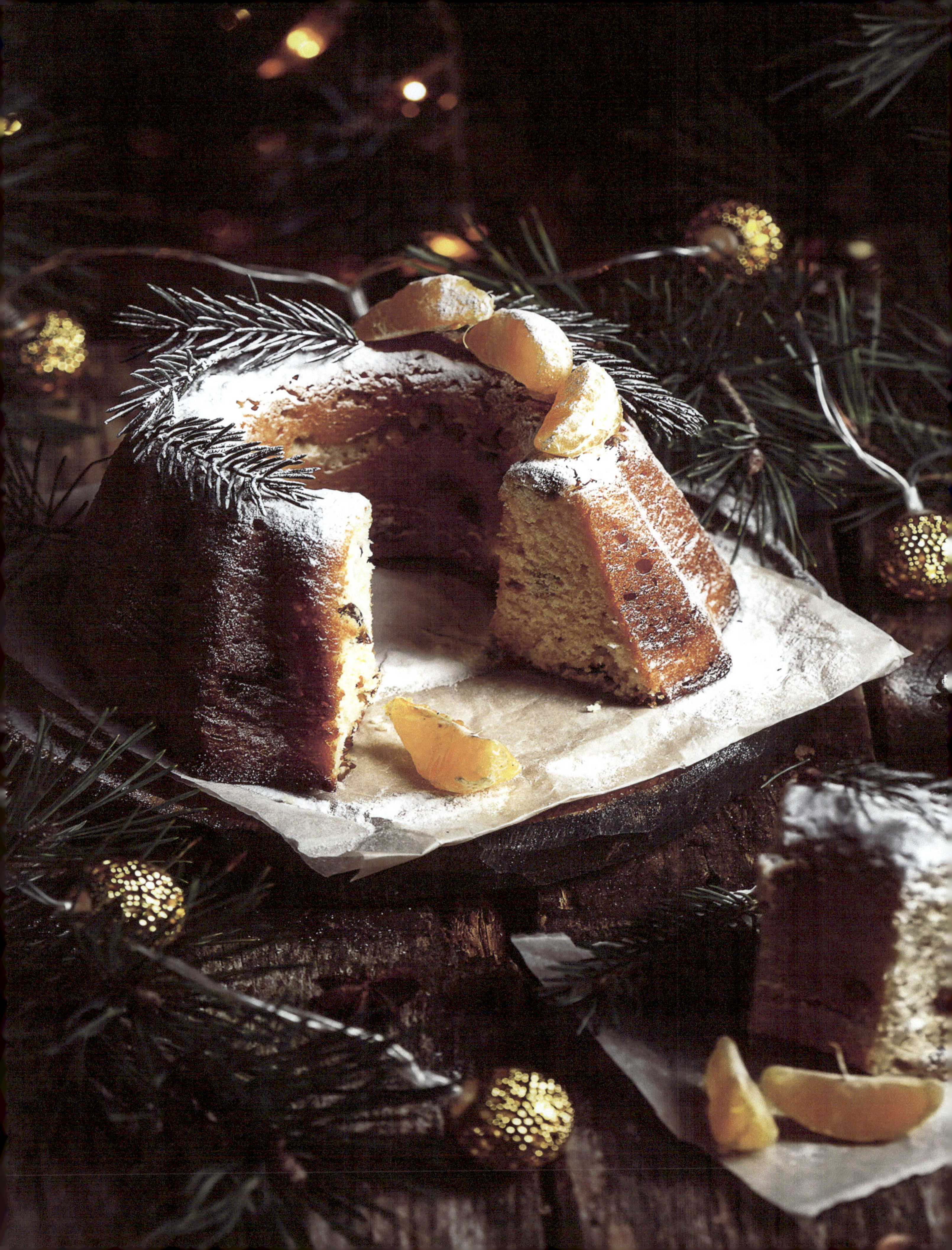

www.ingramcontent.com/pod-product-compliance
Lightning Source LLC
Chambersburg PA
CBHW051826210526
45473CB00005B/1764
* 9 7 9 8 3 0 2 7 2 2 4 5 4 *